christmas hugs

christmas hugs

inspiring sentiments for the festive season

edited by siân keogh

Published in the United States in 2008
by Tangent Publications
an imprint of
Axis Publishing Limited
8c Accommodation Road
London NW11 8ED
www.axispublishing.co.uk

Creative Director: Siân Keogh
Designer: Sean Keogh, Simon De Lotz
Production Manager: Jo Ryan

ISBN: 978-1-904707-84-4

9 8 7 6 5 4 3 2 1

Printed and bound in China

about this book

Offering maximum appeal to a wide variety of people, *christmas hugs* is both a book to keep and a book for giving. It offers a collection of wise, witty, and thought-provoking words and phrases on the subject of Christmas in its widest sense. Complementing the words is a selection of beautiful, evocative, and appealing animal photographs.

Whatever your thoughts on Christmas, you will find here inspiring words and photographs that resonate on the true meaning of the festive season.

about the editor

Siân Keogh has worked in publishing for several years, producing a variety of books on a wide range of subjects. From the many thousands of contributions that were sent to her by people from all around the world and all walks of life, she has compiled a collection to reflect the meaning of Christmas to the widest possible audience.

Christmas is a special day,
spent in a warm circle of family.

Christmas is a race to see
which gives out first—
your money or your feet.

At Christmas the world is young.

The best spirits come
out at Christmas.

The heart of the
season is love.

Love is the true
spirit of Christmas.

At Christmas, all roads lead home.

Giving yourself is the
greatest gift of all.

There are no strangers
on Christmas Eve.

For Christmas decorate
yourself with a smile!

Blessed is the season which
engages the whole world in
a conspiracy of love.

Remember, if Christmas isn't found in your heart, you won't find it under a tree.

It is Christmas in the heart that puts Christmas in the air.

Never worry about the
size of your Christmas tree.
In the eyes of children,
they are all 30 feet tall.

Christmas is sharing.

People are so worried about what they eat between Christmas and the New Year, but they really should be worried about what they eat between the New Year and Christmas.

Christmas is in my heart twelve months a year and thanks to credit cards…

…it's on my bank statement twelve months a year also.

Christmas is love in action.

An old-fashioned
Christmas is hard
to forget.

The spirit of the
season is peace.

Christmas Eve is a night of song.

Selfishness makes Christmas a burden, love makes it a delight.

The simplest things give the greatest glow of happiness.

Christmas makes
everything beautiful.

Snow on Christmas means
Easter will be green.

I wish we could put some of the Christmas spirit in jars and open a jar of it every month.

There's nothing sadder in this world than to awake Christmas morning and not be a child.

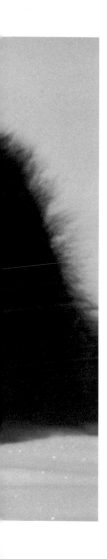

Christmas memories
gather and dance
like snowflakes.

Go-givers will become
the best go-getters.

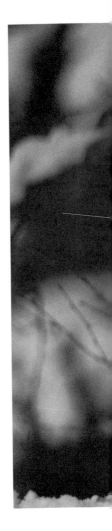

Christmas is a frame of mind.

Once again, we come
to the Holiday Season,
a deeply religious time
that each of us observes,
in his own way, by going
to the mall of his choice.

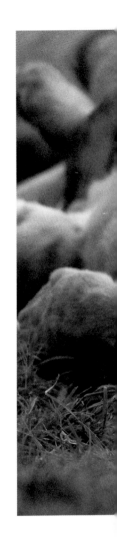

Christmas is loving others.

Anyone who believes
that men are the equal
of women has never seen
a man trying to wrap
a Christmas present.

Christmas is a time
when everybody wants his
past forgotten and his
present remembered.

Christmas waves a magic wand over this world, and behold, everything is softer and more beautiful.

All I want for Christmas is You.

A lovely thing about Christmas is that it's compulsory, and we all go through it together.

Christmas is the
happiness that lights
our children's eyes.

Merry Kissmas
with lots of hugs.

The big man is coming and already I'm shedding a tear...

...I'm just too santamental.

People really act weird at Christmas-time! What other time of year do you sit in front of a dead tree in the living room and eat nuts and sweets out of your socks?

Believe in Santa…

…just beclause!

Christmas is the time
to let your heart
do the thinking.

Christmas is doing a little something extra for someone.

Christmas is the time to remember that love is more valuable than gold.

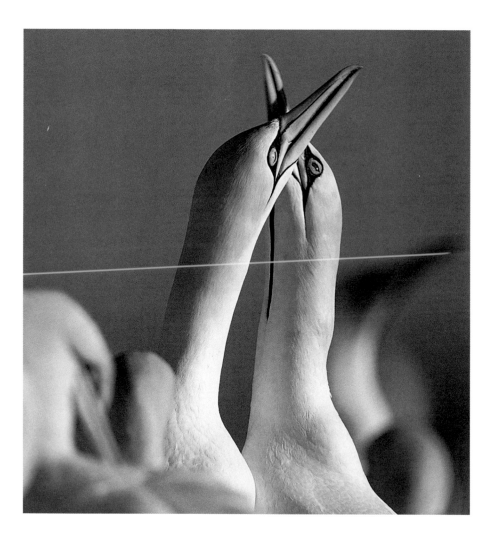

Why does Scrooge love Rudolph
the Red-Nosed Reindeer?

Because every buck is
dear to him.

Christmas is for
defrosting chilled hearts.

May peace be your gift
at Christmas and your blessing
all year through.

I will honor Christmas
in my heart, and try to
keep it all the year.

May the spirit of Christmas bring you peace, the gladness of Christmas give you hope, and the warmth of Christmas grant you love.

A cynic is just a man
who found out when he
was ten that there wasn't any
Santa Claus, and he's still upset.

Seek joy in what
you give…

…not in what you get.

Christmas—that magic blanket that wraps itself about us.

Christmas is a spark
that ignites in
someone's heart.

The warmth and joy of Christmas brings people closer together.

Play and make
good cheer…

…for Christmas
comes but once a year.

One of the most glorious messes in the world is the mess created in the living room on Christmas day.

The message of Christmas
is that the visible material
world is bound to the
invisible spiritual world.

Christmas is hope reborn for peace, for understanding, and for goodwill to men.